3 M[illegible] PORTUGUESE

LESSONS 1 – 3

KIERAN BALL

Mother Dearest...

I'd like to dedicate this book to my mum, who has given me so much in life, as well as life itself.

Thank you for your unequalled support, and thank you for being the one person in the world who has always held unwavering belief in everything I do.

You're the hardest working person I know and you have pushed me to be the greatest version of myself that I can be.

Hello and welcome to "3 Minute Portuguese". I'm Kieran and I'm a language tutor based in the UK and I wrote this book to help you to learn to speak Portuguese.

The lessons in this book are based on the methodology I developed for teaching languages, which I use in all my classes and courses. The methodology will get you speaking quickly, without the struggle normally associated with language learning.

I'll not bore you with my life story or intricate details of the history of the methodology; I know you probably just want to start learning Portuguese now, so I'll let you get on with it.

Actually, I've changed my mind, I will bore you a little before we start. It's my book! I'll keep it as brief as I can though.

I've been tutoring people for over ten years on a one-to-one basis in a range of subjects. I love languages, I love learning and I love teaching. I also love chocolate, but this isn't really the place to discuss my chocoholism. I'm very lucky that I get to teach people every day. However, I can't fit everybody who asks me into my schedule so, regrettably, I end up turning a lot of people away. I wish I could teach the whole world but I'm yet to figure out a way of duplicating myself!

The next best thing is to teach through the medium of a book. So, that's what I've decided to do. If you're reading this book, then I will soon be teaching you the glorious splendour that is the Portuguese language.

Anyway, I'll stop blathering on in a minute and we'll get started with learning. But, firstly, let me just say this...

Hullabaloo!

No, I'm joking, of course, let me say this instead...

We are all human beings, which means we all possess the attributes that make us human beings. There's a wonderful quote by a man called Terence:

"I am human, and nothing that is human is alien to me"

What it means is that if one person is capable of something, then we are all capable of it, because we're all humans too. There's nothing in the world that I cannot understand if somebody before me has succeeded in understanding it. Therefore, it's only logical that since there are more than 260 million people in the world who have managed to learn to speak Portuguese, then you can learn it too!

Anyway, philosophising over. Let's begin.

Contents

LESSON 1

"Portuguese in three minutes?" I hear you cry suspiciously. Yes, this book is intricately designed to get you speaking Portuguese in the shortest time possible.

I've created this book the complete beginner who only has a few minutes to spare each day. I've set out each lesson so that they can be completed in short bursts, whenever you find yourself with a moment of freedom.

Before you start this book, let me share with you an extremely handy learning tip that helped me to progress quickly and effectively in language learning. When most people start studying for anything, they tend to spend the first day or two studying for hours and hours and get through loads of work, however, very quickly this begins to dwindle. You might feel like spending hours studying Portuguese, which is great, but you want that feeling of motivation to continue but it won't continue if you actually spend hours studying. Limit your study time to chunks of just three minutes. No more!

If you limit your studying to just three minute chunks, there are three things that will happen:

1. You'll maintain your enthusiasm

If you want to learn anything, you have to maintain enthusiasm or else you won't continue. If you limit your study time to just three minutes, you'll keep Portuguese fresh and exciting and you'll be eager to learn. If you spend hours studying, very quickly you'll get bored with Portuguese and it'll turn into a chore.

2. You'll study more consistently

It's much better to study for just three minutes once a day than to study for three hours once a week. A spare three minutes is relatively easy to find even in the most hectic of schedules. If you make sure you complete at least one three minute study session every day, it'll quickly become a habit that you'll do without thinking. It's much easier to fit in a daily three minute habit than a weekly one hour habit. By doing this, you'll become a much more consistent learner and consistency is the key to success.

3. You'll remember things better

This is my favourite reason as to why you should limit your study to just three minute chunks. If you study something for just three minutes every day, you'll trick your brain into memorising the information more quickly than if it were to see the information for hours each day. It'll think, "I see this information every day so it must be important, but I don't see it for very long so I'd better hold onto it and make it into a memory fast!" You'll be amazed at how much more easily things tend to stay in your brain if you limit yourself to just three minutes a day.

So, three minutes is the key! Set a timer, and once you reach three minutes, stop. Then give yourself at least half an hour before you do another three minutes. You should aim to do at least one three minute chunk every day, any more than that is a bonus, but one is fine. Just read through this book and complete the exercises, that's all. You'll be amazed at how much you learn.

Here's your first word in Portuguese:

bom

It means "good"
You pronounce it "bon(g)"
I've put the (g) in brackets because you say this word like you say the word "bong" but you don't say the 'g' at all. You can't even hear the 'n'

Here's your next word:

é

It means "it is"
You pronounce it "ay"

How would you say this in Portuguese?

It is good.

It is good.

É bom.

You'll start to notice similarities between Portuguese and English words:

fantástico

It means "fantastic"

You pronounce it "fan-tash-tee-koo"

WORD LIST SO FAR

bom - *good*
é - *it is*
fantástico - *fantastic*

How would you say this in Portuguese?

It is fantastic.

It is fantastic.

É fantástico.

é fantástico

You might be wondering what that little line is on top of the á and the é.

It's called an accent. Don't worry about them too much for the time being; we'll look at them in detail in a later lesson. For now, just remember that they're there.

Here's another word that looks similar to English:

absolutamente

It means "absolutely"
You pronounce it "ab-so-loo-ta-men-tuh"

How would you say this in Portuguese?

It is absolutely fantastic.

It is absolutely fantastic.

É absolutamente fantástico.

WORD LIST SO FAR

bom - *good*
é - *it is*
fantástico - *fantastic*
absolutamente - *absolutely*

Here's a cute little Portuguese word:

aqui

It means "here"
You pronounce it "a-key"

How would you say these three sentences in Portuguese?

It is good here.

It's fantastic here.

It's absolutely fantastic here.

It is good here.
É bom aqui.

It's fantastic here.
É fantástico aqui.

It's absolutely fantastic here.
É absolutamente fantástico aqui.

Here's a word you might recognize if you've learnt any Portuguese before:

muito

It means "very"

You pronounce it "mwee-tooh"

WORD LIST SO FAR

bom - *good*
é - *it is*
fantástico - *fantastic*
absolutamente – *absolutely*
aqui – *here*
muito - *very*

How would you say these two sentences in Portuguese?

It is very good.

It's very good here.

It is very good.
É muito bom.

It is very good here.
É muito bom aqui.

The word "é" means "it is", well, here's the opposite:

não é

It means "it isn't"
You pronounce it "now ay"

WORD LIST SO FAR

bom - *good*
é - *it is*
fantástico - *fantastic*
absolutamente – *absolutely*
aqui – *here*
muito - *very*
não é – *it isn't*

How would you say the following in Portuguese?

It isn't good.

It isn't very good.

It isn't fantastic.

It isn't very good here.

It isn't good.
Não é bom.

It isn't very good.
Não é muito bom.

It isn't fantastic.
Não é fantástico.

It isn't very good here.
Não é muito bom aqui.

You've learnt quite a few words and phrases in Portuguese now, and you've hopefully been saying them out loud so that you can master the pronunciation. Now, to really embed these words and phrases in your brain, let's do some translations.

I've put some sentences in English below. Try and work out how to say them in Portuguese, and then check to see if you got it right by checking the answers at the bottom of the page.

1. It's good
2. It's absolutely fantastic here
3. It's good here
4. It is very good
5. It isn't good here
6. It isn't good; it's fantastic
7. It's fantastic
8. It's fantastic here
9. It isn't good here; it's absolutely fantastic
10. It's very good here

1. É bom
2. É absolutamente fantástico aqui
3. É bom aqui
4. É muito bom
5. Não é bom aqui
6. Não é bom ; é fantástico
7. É fantástico
8. É fantástico aqui
9. Não é bom aqui ; é absolutamente fantástico
10. É muito bom aqui

Now, let's have a go at doing some reverse translations. Try and work out what these Portuguese sentences mean in English, then check the answers underneath to see if you were correct.

1. Não é muito bom
2. É muito bom
3. Não é fantástico aqui
4. É absolutamente fantástico aqui
5. Não é muito bom aqui
6. É bom
7. É fantástico aqui
8. Não é bom aqui
9. É bom aqui
10. Não é bom ; é absolutamente fantástico

1. It isn't very good
2. It's very good
3. It isn't fantastic here
4. It's absolutely fantastic here
5. It isn't very good here
6. It's good
7. It's fantastic here
8. It isn't good here
9. It's good here
10. It isn't good; it's absolutely fantastic

Let’s recap the words we’ve learnt in this lesson. How did you say these words in Portuguese?

it is

absolutely

fantastic

good

here

very

it isn’t

it is	é
absolutely	absolutamente
fantastic	fantástico
good	bom
here	aqui
very	muito
it isn’t	não é

What else?

There is plenty you can do to ensure the language stays firmly in your brain and doesn't disappear. You can play about with building sentences from the words you've learnt so far. Whenever you find yourself with a spare 30 seconds, think of something you can say in Portuguese. Saying short sentences to yourself in Portuguese throughout the day keeps the language at the forefront of your mind.

Also, from time to time, there will be a word or two (or maybe three) that just will not stay in your memory no matter how hard you try. What you should do to overcome this is write the word down in English in big letters in the middle of a blank piece of paper. Put the piece of paper in your pocket and take it out a few times each day. Whenever you take it out, look at the English word and say the Portuguese word to yourself along with a Portuguese sentence that contains this word. The first few times, you might struggle to think of what the Portuguese word is and you'll have to double check. However, pretty quickly, you'll remember the Portuguese without having to check. You'll be amazed at how well this technique works.

Finally, before I end this first lesson, I'll just give you some information on what it means to learn a language. Memorising lots of words isn't what it means to learn a language. It's a start but it isn't going to get you very far. What you need to be able to do is put those words together to get your thoughts and ideas across to somebody else.

Each time you learn a new word, think to yourself, "Where could I use this?" Make up a sentence and think about where you could say it. "É muito bom" - you could say this to a waiter in a restaurant when he asks you how your meal is.

By doing this, you're giving the words relevance in your life. You'll remember things much more easily if you can see where it's going to be useful. Also, by building sentences, you're subconsciously creating a list of things to say so that you'll never be lost for words.

Even when you're in Portugal you can do this. Before entering a restaurant, for example, have a quick think about what you could say to the waiter when you go inside. This helps to build your confidence and stops you from having to think on the spot. You'll be more likely to speak if you have already prepared something to say.

LESSON 2

Let's start this lesson with a quick recap of the words and phrases we learnt in the last lesson. How do you say the following in Portuguese?

absolutely
it isn't
good
fantastic
very
it is
here

If there are any words you can't remember, go back to the last lesson and have a quick review of them before you start this lesson. It's really important that you remember the words you've learnt so far before you move on to learn any more.

Here's your first word in Portuguese for this lesson:

delicioso

It means "delicious"
You pronounce it "deli-see-oh-zoo"

How would you say this in Portuguese?

It is delicious.

It is delicious.

É delicioso.

Here's your next word in Portuguese:

extraordinário

It means "extraordinary"
You pronounce it "ekshtra-or-di-na-reoo"

WORD LIST SO FAR

delicioso - *delicious*
extraordinário - *extraordinary*

How would you say these three sentences in Portuguese?

It is extraordinary.

It is absolutely extraordinary.

It is absolutely extraordinary here.

It is extraordinary.
É extraordinário.

It is absolutely extraordinary.
É absolutamente extraordinário.

It is absolutely extraordinary here.
É absolutamente extraordinário aqui.

Here's a beautiful little word in Portuguese:

lindo

It means "beautiful"
You pronounce it "lin-doo"

WORD LIST SO FAR

delicioso - *delicious*
extraordinário - *extraordinary*
lindo - *beautiful*

How would you say the following in Portuguese?

It is beautiful.

It is very beautiful.

It is very beautiful here.

It is absolutely beautiful here.

It is beautiful.
É lindo.

It is very beautiful.
É muito lindo.

It is very beautiful here.
É muito lindo aqui.

It is absolutely beautiful here.
É absolutamente lindo aqui.

Here's a useful phrase in Portuguese:

para mim

It means "for me"
You pronounce it "pa-ra min(g)"
Again, I've put the 'g' in brackets because you say the word "mim" like the word "ming" without the 'g'

WORD LIST SO FAR

delicioso - *delicious*
extraordinário - *extraordinary*
lindo - *beautiful*
para mim – *for me*

How would you say these sentences in Portuguese?

It is for me.

It isn’t for me.

It isn’t good for me.

It isn’t very good for me.

It is for me.
É para mim.

It isn't for me.
Não é para mim.

It isn't good for me.
Não é bom para mim.

It isn't very good for me.
Não é muito bom para mim.

The phrase "para mim" actually has two meanings in Portuguese. We've seen it can mean "for me" but, if you put "para mim" at the start of a sentence in Portuguese, it can mean "in my opinion" or "I think":

para mim

It means "in my opinion" or "I think"
You pronounce it "pa-ra min(g)"

WORD LIST SO FAR

delicioso - *delicious*
extraordinário - *extraordinary*
lindo - *beautiful*
para mim – *for me*
para mim – *I think / in my opinion*

How would you say these five things in Portuguese?

I think it is good.

I think it's very good.

I think it's delicious.

I think it's absolutely extraordinary here.

I think it's fantastic here.

I think it's good.
Para mim, é bom.

I think it's very good.
Para mim, é muito bom.

I think it's delicious.
Para mim, é delicioso.

I think it's absolutely extraordinary here.
Para mim, é absolutamente extraordinário aqui.

I think it's fantastic here.
Para mim, é fantástico aqui.

Now we've added quite a few new words to our Portuguese repertoire, let's practise putting them together into sentences. How do you say these sentences in Portuguese?

1. It's very beautiful here
2. It's absolutely beautiful
3. I think it's very good
4. It's absolutely extraordinary here
5. It isn't for me
6. It isn't very good for me
7. It isn't good; it's absolutely extraordinary
8. It's absolutely delicious
9. I think it's delicious
10. I think it's fantastic

1. É muito lindo aqui
2. É absolutamente lindo
3. Para mim, é muito bom
4. É absolutamente extraordinário aqui
5. Não é para mim
6. Não é muito bom para mim
7. Não é bom; é absolutamente extraordinário
8. É absolutamente delicioso
9. Para mim, é delicioso
10. Para mim, é fantástico

Now, let's have a go at doing some reverse translations. What do these Portuguese sentences mean in English?

1. É extraordinário
2. É absolutamente lindo
3. Para mim, é absolutamente lindo aqui
4. Para mim, é bom
5. É muito bom para mim
6. Não é para mim
7. É delicioso
8. Para mim, é delicioso
9. É absolutamente lindo aqui
10. Não é muito lindo

1. It's extraordinary
2. It's absolutely beautiful
3. I think it's absolutely beautiful here
4. I think it's good
5. It's very good for me
6. It isn't for me
7. It's delicious
8. I think it's delicious
9. It's absolutely beautiful here
10. It isn't very beautiful

What we're going to do now are some recap translations, which will incorporate words we learnt in the previous lesson.

1. It isn't very good
2. It isn't good here
3. It's absolutely fantastic here
4. It's fantastic
5. It's good here
6. It's very good here
7. It's fantastic here
8. It isn't good here; it's absolutely fantastic
9. It isn't very good here
10. It's very good

1. Não é muito bom
2. Não é bom aqui
3. É absolutamente fantástico aqui
4. É fantástico
5. É bom aqui
6. É muito bom aqui
7. É fantástico aqui
8. Não é bom aqui; é absolutamente fantástico
9. Não é muito bom aqui
10. É muito bom

Let's now do some Portuguese to English recap translations.

1. Não é bom aqui
2. Não é muito bom aqui
3. É muito bom aqui
4. É fantástico aqui
5. Não é bom aqui; é absolutamente fantástico
6. É absolutamente fantástico aqui
7. Não é fantástico
8. É bom aqui
9. É bom
10. É fantástico

1. It isn't good here
2. It isn't very good here
3. It's very good here
4. It's fantastic here
5. It isn't good here; it's absolutely fantastic
6. It's absolutely fantastic here
7. It isn't fantastic
8. It's good here
9. It's good
10. It's fantastic

Let's recap all the words we've learnt so far. How did you say these words in Portuguese?

1. it is
2. here
3. fantastic
4. delicious
5. it isn't
6. good
7. very
8. extraordinary
9. I think
10. beautiful
11. for me
12. absolutely

1. é
2. aqui
3. fantástico
4. delicioso
5. não é
6. bom
7. muito
8. extraordinário
9. para mim
10. lindo
11. para mim
12. absolutamente

LESSON 3

Let's start this lesson with a quick recap of the words and phrases we learnt in the last lesson. How do you say the following in Portuguese?

for me
I think
delicious
extraordinary
beautiful

If there are any words you can't remember, go back to the last lesson and have a quick review of them before you start this lesson. It's really important that you remember the words you've learnt so far before you move on to learn any more.

Here's your first word in Portuguese for this lesson:

mas

It means "but"

You pronounce it "mash"

How would you say this in Portuguese?

It is delicious but it isn’t very good for me.

It is delicious but it isn't very good for me.

É delicioso mas não é muito bom para mim.

Here's your next word in Portuguese:

sim

It means "yes"

You pronounce it "sin(g)"

You say it sort of like the word "sing" but without the 'g' on the end

WORD LIST SO FAR

mas - *but*
sim - *yes*

How would you say these few sentences in Portuguese?

Yes, it's for me.

Yes, it's absolutely delicious.

Yes, I think it's good.

Yes, it's for me.
Sim, é para mim.

Yes, it's absolutely delicious.
Sim, é absolutamente delicioso.

Yes, I think it's good.
Sim, para mim, é bom.

Here's a common yet useful word in Portuguese:

obrigado

It means "thank you" or "thanks"
You pronounce it "ob-ree-gah-doo"

thank you

In Portuguese, the word for "thank you" is "obrigado". However, if you're a woman, you change it slightly to "obrigada".

If you get this wrong, it's not the end of the world; you'll still be understood. Just try to remember that, if you're a man, you should say 'obrigado' and if you're a woman, you should say 'obrigada'.

How would you say the sentences below in Portuguese?

Yes, thank you, it's delicious.

Yes, thank you, it's fantastic.

It's very good, thanks.

Yes, it is for me, thank you.

Yes, thank you, it's delicious.
Sim, obrigado, é delicioso.

Yes, thank you, it's fantastic.
Sim, obrigado, é fantástico.

It's very good, thanks.
Sim, é muito bom, obrigado.

Yes, it's for me, thank you.
Sim, é para mim, obrigado.

Here's a new word for you:

sempre

It means "always"
You pronounce it "saym-pruh"

WORD LIST SO FAR

mas - *but*
sim - *yes*
obrigado / obrigada – *thank you*
sempre – *always*

How would you say these sentences in Portuguese?

It is always fantastic here.

It isn't always very good here.

I think it's always beautiful here.

It's always absolutely delicious.

It is always fantastic here.
É sempre fantástico aqui.

It isn't always very good here.
Não é sempre muito bom aqui.

I think it's always beautiful here.
Para mim, é sempre lindo aqui.

It's always absolutely delicious.
É sempre absolutamente delicioso.

Here's a perfect little word in Portuguese:

perfeito

It means "perfect"
You pronounce it "pair-fay-too"

WORD LIST SO FAR

mas - *but*
sim - *yes*
obrigado / obrigada – *thank you*
sempre – *always*
perfeito – *perfect*

How would you say the five sentences below in Portuguese?

Yes, it's perfect, thank you.

I think it's perfect.

It's absolutely perfect.

I think it's absolutely perfect here.

It's always perfect here.

Yes, it's perfect, thank you.
Sim, é perfeito, obrigado.

I think it's perfect.
Para mim, é perfeito.

It's absolutely perfect.
É absolutamente perfeito.

I think it's absolutely perfect here.
Para mim, é absolutamente perfeito aqui.

It's always perfect here.
É sempre perfeito aqui.

Here's a useful word in Portuguese:

isso

It means "that"
You pronounce it "iss-oo"

<u>WORD LIST SO FAR</u>

mas - *but*
sim - *yes*
obrigado / obrigada – *thank you*
sempre – *always*
perfeito – *perfect*
isso – *that*

How would you say this in Portuguese?

That for me.

That for me.

Isso para mim.

If you put the word “isso” in front of the word “é” you get:

isso é

It means “that is”
You pronounce it “iss-oo ay”

WORD LIST SO FAR

mas - *but*
sim - *yes*
obrigado / obrigada – *thank you*
sempre – *always*
perfeito – *perfect*
isso – *that*
isso é – *that is*

Finally, how would you say the five sentences below in Portuguese?

That is good.

That is very good.

That is absolutely fantastic.

That is for me.

I think that is perfect.

That is good.

Isso é bom.

That is very good.

Isso é muito bom.

That is absolutely fantastic.

Isso é absolutamente bom.

That is for me.

Isso é para mim.

I think that is perfect.

Para mim, isso é perfeito.

It's time to practise what we've learnt in this lesson.

1. It's always perfect here
2. It isn't always perfect here
3. It's always absolutely fantastic here
4. It's for me, thank you
5. Yes, it's for me
6. It isn't always good here
7. It's always very good
8. I think that is absolutely perfect
9. That is delicious but it isn't very good for me
10. Yes, it's perfect, thank you

1. É sempre perfeito aqui
2. Não é sempre perfeito aqui
3. É sempre absolutamente fantástico aqui
4. É para mim, obrigado
5. Sim, é para mim
6. Não é sempre bom aqui
7. É sempre muito bom
8. Para mim, isso é absolutamente perfeito
9. Isso é delicioso mas não é muito bom para mim
10. Sim, é perfeito, obrigado

Now, let's have a go at doing some reverse translations.

1. Sim, obrigado
2. É absolutamente perfeito
3. Não é fantástico mas é muito bom
4. Para mim, é perfeito
5. É sempre absolutamente fantástico aqui
6. Para mim, é absolutamente extraordinário
7. É sempre muito bom
8. É sempre muito bom aqui
9. Sim, isso é para mim, obrigado
10. Isso é absolutamente delicioso

1. Yes, thank you
2. It's absolutely perfect
3. It isn't fantastic but it's very good
4. I think it's perfect
5. It's always absolutely fantastic here
6. I think it's absolutely extraordinary
7. It's always very good
8. It's always very good here
9. Yes, that's for me, thank you
10. That is absolutely delicious

What we're going to do now are some recap translations, which will incorporate words we learnt in the previous lessons.

1. It isn't fantastic
2. It's very good here
3. It's good here
4. It's delicious
5. I think it's absolutely beautiful here
6. It isn't very good here
7. It is absolutely fantastic
8. I think it's good
9. It is fantastic
10. It's absolutely extraordinary here

1. Não é fantástico
2. É muito bom aqui
3. É bom aqui
4. É delicioso
5. Para mim, é absolutamente lindo aqui
6. Não é muito bom aqui
7. É absolutamente fantástico
8. Para mim, é bom
9. É fantástico
10. É absolutamente extraordinário aqui

Let's now do some Portuguese to English recap translations.

1. Não é bom
2. Não é muito bom para mim
3. É lindo
4. É fantástico
5. É extraordinário aqui
6. É extraordinário
7. Não é fantástico
8. É muito lindo aqui
9. Não é muito bom aqui
10. Não é muito extraordinário

1. It isn't good
2. It isn't very good for me
3. It's beautiful
4. It's fantastic
5. It's extraordinary here
6. It's extraordinary
7. It isn't fantastic
8. It's very beautiful here
9. It isn't very good here
10. It isn't very extraordinary

Let's recap all the words we've learnt so far. How did you say these words in Portuguese?

1. beautiful
2. thanks
3. here
4. it is
5. yes
6. very
7. for me
8. that
9. always
10. fantastic
11. good
12. absolutely
13. I think
14. perfect
15. extraordinary
16. but
17. it isn't
18. delicious
19. that is...

1. lindo
2. obrigado
3. aqui
4. é
5. sim
6. muito
7. para mim
8. isso
9. sempre
10. fantástico
11. bom
12. absolutamente
13. para mim
14. perfeito
15. extraordinário
16. mas
17. não é
18. delicioso
19. isso é...

Obrigado

Before you go, I'd like to say "obrigado" for buying this book. There are lots of Portuguese books available on Amazon and you chose to read mine, so I am eternally grateful for that.

I hope you have enjoyed this book and I hope you're glad you made the purchase. I also hope you've started to realise how easy learning a new language can be.

This book contained lessons one to three of my "3 Minute Portuguese" course. If you would like to learn more, you can get the next book in the series containing lessons four to six, and further books after that to continue building your Portuguese language skills.

For more information on where to get the next books, or if you'd like any more tips on language learning, you can visit my website www.3minute.club

Thank you again, obrigado e até logo!

30217039R00057

Printed in Great Britain
by Amazon